The
Prayer
MAP®
for Moms

D1710514

BARBOUR
PUBLISHING

Date:

Dear Heavenly Father,
....
....
....
....

My prayer for my kid(s)
today. . .
....
....
....
....
....
....
....
....
....
....
....

Thank You for. . .
....
....
....
....
....
....
....
....
....
....

Worries I need to share with You. . .
....
....
....
....
....

I am overwhelmed. . .

....
....
....
....

I need Your strength. . .

....
....
....
....

Please give me wisdom. . .

....
....
....
....
....
....

Amen. Thank You, Father, for hearing my prayers.

"As a mother comforts her child,
so will I comfort you."
ISAIAH 66:13

Date:

Dear Heavenly Father,

....
....
....
....

My prayer for my kid(s) today. . .

....
....
....
....
....
....
....
....
....

Thank You for. . .

....
....
....
....
....
....
....
....
....
....

Worries I need to share with You. . .

....
....
....
....
....

I am overwhelmed. . .

....

....

....

I need Your strength. . .

....

....

....

....

Please give me wisdom. . .

....

....

....

....

....

Amen. Thank You, Father, for hearing my prayers.

"Can a mother forget the baby at her breast
and have no compassion on the child she
has borne? Though she may forget,
I will not forget you!"
ISAIAH 49:15

Date:

Dear Heavenly Father,
....
....
....
....

My prayer for my kid(s) today. . .
....
....
....
....
....
....
....
....

Thank You for. . .
....
....
....
....
....
....
....
....
....

Worries I need to share with You. . .
....
....
....
....
....

I am overwhelmed. . .

I need Your strength. . .

Please give me wisdom. . .

Amen. Thank You, Father, for hearing my prayers.

She is clothed with strength and dignity;
she can laugh at the days to come.
PROVERBS 31:25

Date:

Dear Heavenly Father,
....
....
....
....

My prayer for my kid(s) today. . .
....
....
....
....
....
....
....
....
....

Thank You for. . .
....
....
....
....
....
....
....
....
....

Worries I need to share with You. . .
....
....
....
....
....

I am overwhelmed. . .

I need Your strength. . .

Please give me wisdom. . .

Amen. Thank You, Father, for hearing my prayers.

*She speaks with wisdom,
and faithful instruction is on her tongue.*
PROVERBS 31:26

Date:

Dear Heavenly Father,

My prayer for my kid(s) today. . .

Thank You for. . .

Worries I need to share with You. . .

I am overwhelmed. . .

I need Your strength. . .

Please give me wisdom. . .

Amen. Thank You, Father, for hearing my prayers.

Her children arise and call her blessed;
her husband also, and he praises her:
"Many women do noble things,
but you surpass them all."

PROVERBS 31:28–29

Date:

Dear Heavenly Father,
....
....
....
....

My prayer for my kid(s) today. . .
....
....
....
....
....
....
....
....
....

Thank You for. . .
....
....
....
....
....
....
....
....
....
....

Worries I need to share with You. . .
....
....
....
....
....

I am overwhelmed. . .

....

....

....

....

I need Your strength. . .

....

....

....

....

Please give me wisdom. . .

....

....

....

....

....

....

Amen. Thank You, Father, for hearing my prayers.

These commandments that I give you today
are to be on your hearts. Impress them on your
children. Talk about them when you sit at home
and when you walk along the road, when
you lie down and when you get up.

DEUTERONOMY 6:6–7

Date:

Dear Heavenly Father,
....
....
....
....

My prayer for my kid(s) today. . .
....
....
....
....
....
....
....
....

Thank You for. . .
....
....
....
....
....
....
....
....
....
....

Worries I need to share with You. . .
....
....
....
....
....

I am overwhelmed. . .

_____

_____

_____

_____

I need Your strength. . .

_____

_____

_____

_____

Please give me wisdom. . .

_____

_____

_____

_____

_____

_____

Amen. Thank You, Father, for hearing my prayers.

*Honor her for all that her hands
have done, and let her works bring
her praise at the city gate.*
PROVERBS 31:31

Date:

Dear Heavenly Father,
....
....
....
....

My prayer for my kid(s) today. . .
....
....
....
....
....
....
....

Thank You for. . .
....
....
....
....
....
....
....
....

Worries I need to share with You. . .
....
....
....
....
....

I am overwhelmed. . .

....

....

....

I need Your strength. . .

....

....

....

....

Please give me wisdom. . .

....

....

....

....

....

....

Amen. Thank You, Father, for hearing my prayers.

*For you created my inmost being; you knit
me together in my mother's womb. I praise you
because I am fearfully and wonderfully made;
your works are wonderful, I know that full well.*

PSALM 139:13–14

Date:

Dear Heavenly Father,

My prayer for my kid(s) today. . .

Thank You for. . .

Worries I need to share with You. . .

I am overwhelmed. . .

I need Your strength. . .

Please give me wisdom. . .

Amen. Thank You, Father, for hearing my prayers.

"Everyone who quotes proverbs will quote this
proverb about you: 'Like mother, like daughter.' "
EZEKIEL 16:44

Date:

Dear Heavenly Father,
....
....
....
....

My prayer for my kid(s) today. . .
....
....
....
....
....
....
....
....

Thank You for. . .
....
....
....
....
....
....
....
....

Worries I need to share with You. . .
....
....
....
....
....

I am overwhelmed. . .

I need Your strength. . .

Please give me wisdom. . .

Amen. Thank You, Father, for hearing my prayers.

Adam named his wife Eve, because she
would become the mother of all the living.
GENESIS 3:20

Date:

Dear Heavenly Father,
....
....
....
....

My prayer for my kid(s) today...
....
....
....
....
....
....
....
....

Thank You for...
....
....
....
....
....
....
....
....
....

Worries I need to share with You...
....
....
....
....

I am overwhelmed. . .

....

....

....

....

I need Your strength. . .

....

....

....

....

Please give me wisdom. . .

....

....

....

....

....

....

Amen. Thank You, Father, for hearing my prayers.

*Your beauty should not come from outward
adornment. . . . Rather, it should be that of your
inner self, the unfading beauty of a gentle and
quiet spirit, which is of great worth in God's sight.*
1 PETER 3:3–4

Date:

Dear Heavenly Father,
....
....
....
....

My prayer for my kid(s) today. . .
....
....
....
....
....
....
....
....
....
....
....

Thank You for. . .
....
....
....
....
....
....
....
....
....
....

Worries I need to share with You. . .
....
....
....
....
....

I am overwhelmed. . .

....

....

....

....

I need Your strength. . .

....

....

....

Please give me wisdom. . .

....

....

....

....

....

....

Amen. Thank You, Father, for hearing my prayers.

Love is patient, love is kind.
1 CORINTHIANS 13:4

Date:

Dear Heavenly Father,
....
....
....
....

My prayer for my kid(s) today. . .
....
....
....
....
....
....
....
....
....

Thank You for. . .
....
....
....
....
....
....
....
....
....

Worries I need to share with You. . .
....
....
....
....
....

I am overwhelmed. . .

I need Your strength. . .

Please give me wisdom. . .

Amen. Thank You, Father, for hearing my prayers.

[Love] always protects, always trusts,
always hopes, always perseveres.
1 CORINTHIANS 13:7

Date: _____

Dear Heavenly Father, _____
_____
_____
_____
_____

My prayer for my kid(s) today. . .
_____
_____
_____
_____
_____
_____

Thank You for. . .
_____
_____
_____
_____
_____
_____
_____
_____
_____

Worries I need to share with You. . .
_____
_____
_____
_____
_____

I am overwhelmed. . .

I need Your strength. . .

Please give me wisdom. . .

Amen. Thank You, Father, for hearing my prayers.

*And now these three remain: faith, hope
and love. But the greatest of these is love.*
1 CORINTHIANS 13:13

Dear Heavenly Father,

My prayer for my kid(s) today. . .

Thank You for. . .

Worries I need to share with You. . .

I am overwhelmed. . .

....
....
....
....

I need Your strength. . .

....
....
....
....

Please give me wisdom. . .

....
....
....
....
....
....

Amen. Thank You, Father, for hearing my prayers.

"My command is this: Love each
other as I have loved you."
JOHN 15:12

Date:

Dear Heavenly Father,
....
....
....
....
....

My prayer for my kid(s) today. . .
....
....
....
....
....
....
....
....
....
....

Thank You for. . .
....
....
....
....
....
....
....
....
....
....

Worries I need to share with You. . .
....
....
....
....
....

I am overwhelmed. . .

I need Your strength. . .

Please give me wisdom. . .

Amen. Thank You, Father, for hearing my prayers.

We love because he first loved us.
1 JOHN 4:19

Date:

Dear Heavenly Father,
....
....
....
....

My prayer for my kid(s)
today. . .
....
....
....
....
....
....
....
....
....
....
....

Thank You for. . .
....
....
....
....
....
....
....
....
....
....
....

Worries I need to share with You. . .
....
....
....
....
....

I am overwhelmed. . .

....
....
....
....

I need Your strength. . .

....
....
....
....

Please give me wisdom. . .

....
....
....
....
....
....

Amen. Thank You, Father, for hearing my prayers.

*Let no debt remain outstanding, except the
continuing debt to love one another.*
ROMANS 13:8

Date:

Dear Heavenly Father,
....
....
....
....

My prayer for my kid(s) today. . .
....
....
....
....
....
....
....
....

Thank You for. . .
....
....
....
....
....
....
....
....
....

Worries I need to share with You. . .
....
....
....
....
....

I am overwhelmed. . .

I need Your strength. . .

Please give me wisdom. . .

Amen. Thank You, Father, for hearing my prayers.

No one has ever seen God; but if we
love one another, God lives in us and
his love is made complete in us.
1 JOHN 4:12

Date:

Dear Heavenly Father,

My prayer for my kid(s) today. . .

Thank You for. . .

Worries I need to share with You. . .

I am overwhelmed. . .

I need Your strength. . .

Please give me wisdom. . .

Amen. Thank You, Father, for hearing my prayers.

Let the morning bring me word of your unfailing love, for I have put my trust in you. Show me the way I should go, for to you I entrust my life.
PSALM 143:8

Date:

Dear Heavenly Father,
....
....
....
....

My prayer for my kid(s) today. . .
....
....
....
....
....
....
....
....
....

Thank You for. . .
....
....
....
....
....
....
....
....
....
....

Worries I need to share with You. . .
....
....
....
....
....

I am overwhelmed. . .

I need Your strength. . .

Please give me wisdom. . .

Amen. Thank You, Father, for hearing my prayers.

But the fruit of the Spirit is love, joy,
peace, forbearance, kindness, goodness,
faithfulness, gentleness and self-control.
Against such things there is no law.

GALATIANS 5:22–23

Date:

Dear Heavenly Father,

My prayer for my kid(s) today. . .

Thank You for. . .

Worries I need to share with You. . .

I am overwhelmed. . .

....

....

....

....

I need Your strength. . .

....

....

....

....

Please give me wisdom. . .

....

....

....

....

....

....

Amen. Thank You, Father, for hearing my prayers.

"Honor your father and your mother,
so that you may live long in the land
the LORD your God is giving you."

EXODUS 20:12

Date:

Dear Heavenly Father,
....
....
....
....

My prayer for my kid(s) today. . .
....
....
....
....
....
....
....
....
....
....

Thank You for. . .
....
....
....
....
....
....
....
....
....
....

Worries I need to share with You. . .
....
....
....
....
....

I am overwhelmed. . .

I need Your strength. . .

Please give me wisdom. . .

Amen. Thank You, Father, for hearing my prayers.

Children are a heritage from the LORD,
offspring a reward from him.
PSALM 127:3

Date:

Dear Heavenly Father,
....
....
....
....

My prayer for my kid(s) today. . .
....
....
....
....
....
....
....

Thank You for. . .
....
....
....
....
....
....
....
....

Worries I need to share with You. . .
....
....
....
....
....

I am overwhelmed. . .

I need Your strength. . .

Please give me wisdom. . .

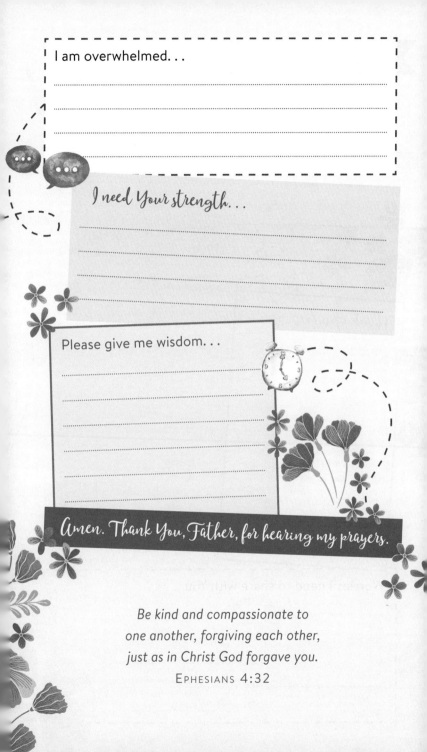

Amen. Thank You, Father, for hearing my prayers.

Be kind and compassionate to
one another, forgiving each other,
just as in Christ God forgave you.
EPHESIANS 4:32

Date:

Dear Heavenly Father,
....
....
....
....

My prayer for my kid(s) today. . .
....
....
....
....
....
....
....
....
....

Thank You for. . .
....
....
....
....
....
....
....
....
....

Worries I need to share with You. . .
....
....
....
....
....

I am overwhelmed. . .

I need Your strength. . .

Please give me wisdom. . .

Amen. Thank You, Father, for hearing my prayers.

Listen. . .to your father's instruction and do not forsake your mother's teaching. They are a garland to grace your head and a chain to adorn your neck.

PROVERBS 1:8–9

Date:

Dear Heavenly Father, ...
....
....
....
....

My prayer for my kid(s) today. . .
....
....
....
....
....
....
....
....
....
....
....
....

Thank You for. . .
....
....
....
....
....
....
....
....
....
....

Worries I need to share with You. . .
....
....
....
....
....

I am overwhelmed. . .

I need Your strength. . .

Please give me wisdom. . .

Amen. Thank You, Father, for hearing my prayers.

*Start children off on the way they
should go, and even when they are
old they will not turn from it.*
PROVERBS 22:6

Date:

Dear Heavenly Father,
....
....
....
....

My prayer for my kid(s) today. . .
....
....
....
....
....
....
....
....
....
....

Thank You for. . .
....
....
....
....
....
....
....
....
....
....

Worries I need to share with You. . .
....
....
....
....
....

I am overwhelmed. . .

....
....
....
....

I need Your strength. . .

....
....
....
....

Please give me wisdom. . .

....
....
....
....
....
....

Amen. Thank You, Father, for hearing my prayers.

May your father and mother rejoice;
may she who gave you birth be joyful!

PROVERBS 23:25

Date:

Dear Heavenly Father,
....
....
....
....

My prayer for my kid(s) today. . .
....
....
....
....
....
....
....
....

Thank You for. . .
....
....
....
....
....
....
....
....

Worries I need to share with You. . .
....
....
....
....
....

I am overwhelmed. . .

I need Your strength. . .

Please give me wisdom. . .

Amen. Thank You, Father, for hearing my prayers.

"Believe in the Lord Jesus, and you
will be saved—you and your household."
ACTS 16:31

Date:

Dear Heavenly Father,

My prayer for my kid(s) today. . .

Thank You for. . .

Worries I need to share with You. . .

I am overwhelmed. . .

....
....
....
....
....

I need Your strength. . .

....
....
....
....

Please give me wisdom. . .

....
....
....
....
....
....

Amen. Thank You, Father, for hearing my prayers.

*How good and pleasant it is when
God's people live together in unity!*

PSALM 133:1

Date:

Dear Heavenly Father,
....
....
....
....

My prayer for my kid(s) today. . .
....
....
....
....
....
....
....
....
....

Thank You for. . .
....
....
....
....
....
....
....
....
....

Worries I need to share with You. . .
....
....
....
....
....

I am overwhelmed. . .

....

....

....

....

I need Your strength. . .

....

....

....

....

Please give me wisdom. . .

....

....

....

....

....

Amen. Thank You, Father, for hearing my prayers.

*I have no greater joy than to hear that
my children are walking in the truth.*
3 JOHN 1:4

Date:

Dear Heavenly Father,
....
....
....
....

My prayer for my kid(s) today. . .
....
....
....
....
....
....
....
....
....

Thank You for. . .
....
....
....
....
....
....
....
....
....
....

Worries I need to share with You. . .
....
....
....
....
....

I am overwhelmed. . .

_____

_____

_____

_____

I need Your strength. . .

_____

_____

_____

_____

Please give me wisdom. . .

_____

_____

_____

_____

_____

_____

Amen. Thank You, Father, for hearing my prayers.

_And Mary said: "My soul glorifies the Lord and my
spirit rejoices in God my Savior, for he has been
mindful of the humble state of his servant. From
now on all generations will call me blessed."_

LUKE 1:46–48

Date:

Dear Heavenly Father, ...
....
....
....
....

My prayer for my kid(s) today. . .
....
....
....
....
....
....
....
....
....

Thank You for. . .
....
....
....
....
....
....
....
....

Worries I need to share with You. . .
....
....
....
....
....

I am overwhelmed. . .

I need Your strength. . .

Please give me wisdom. . .

Amen. Thank You, Father, for hearing my prayers.

"Assemble the people before me to hear my words so
that they may learn to revere me as long as they live
in the land and may teach them to their children."

DEUTERONOMY 4:10

Date:

Dear Heavenly Father,
....
....
....
....

Thank You for...
....
....
....
....
....
....
....
....
....

My prayer for my kid(s) today...
....
....
....
....
....
....
....
....
....
....

Worries I need to share with You...
....
....
....
....
....

I am overwhelmed. . .

I need Your strength. . .

Please give me wisdom. . .

Amen. Thank You, Father, for hearing my prayers.

*I am reminded of your sincere faith, which first
lived in your grandmother Lois and in your mother
Eunice and, I am persuaded, now lives in you also.*

2 TIMOTHY 1:5

Date:

Dear Heavenly Father,

....
....
....
....

My prayer for my kid(s) today. . .

....
....
....
....
....
....
....
....
....

Thank You for. . .

....
....
....
....
....
....
....
....
....

Worries I need to share with You. . .

....
....
....
....
....

I am overwhelmed. . .

I need Your strength. . .

Please give me wisdom. . .

Amen. Thank You, Father, for hearing my prayers.

Above all, love each other deeply,
because love covers over a multitude of sins.
1 PETER 4:8

Date:

Dear Heavenly Father,
....
....
....
....

My prayer for my kid(s) today. . .
....
....
....
....
....
....
....
....
....

Thank You for. . .
....
....
....
....
....
....
....
....
....
....

Worries I need to share with You. . .
....
....
....
....
....

I am overwhelmed. . .

....
....
....
....

I need Your strength. . .

....
....
....
....

Please give me wisdom. . .

....
....
....
....
....

Amen. Thank You, Father, for hearing my prayers.

Be joyful in hope, patient in
affliction, faithful in prayer.
ROMANS 12:12

Date:

Dear Heavenly Father,
....
....
....
....
....

My prayer for my kid(s) today. . .
....
....
....
....
....
....
....
....
....
....
....

Thank You for. . .
....
....
....
....
....
....
....
....
....
....

Worries I need to share with You. . .
....
....
....
....
....

I am overwhelmed. . .

I need Your strength. . .

Please give me wisdom. . .

Amen. Thank You, Father, for hearing my prayers.

The wise woman builds her house.

PROVERBS 14:1

Date:

Dear Heavenly Father,

My prayer for my kid(s) today. . .

Thank You for. . .

Worries I need to share with You. . .

I am overwhelmed. . .

I need Your strength. . .

Please give me wisdom. . .

Amen. Thank You, Father, for hearing my prayers.

A kindhearted woman gains honor.
PROVERBS 11:16

Date:

Dear Heavenly Father,
....
....
....
....

My prayer for my kid(s) today. . .
....
....
....
....
....
....
....
....
....
....

Thank You for. . .
....
....
....
....
....
....
....
....
....
....
....

Worries I need to share with You. . .
....
....
....
....
....

I am overwhelmed. . .

I need Your strength. . .

Please give me wisdom. . .

Amen. Thank You, Father, for hearing my prayers.

_Whatever is true, whatever is noble, whatever
is right, whatever is pure, whatever is lovely,
whatever is admirable—if anything is excellent
or praiseworthy—think about such things._

PHILIPPIANS 4:8

Date:

Dear Heavenly Father, ...
....
....
....
....

My prayer for my kid(s) today. . .
....
....
....
....
....
....
....
....
....

Thank You for. . .
....
....
....
....
....
....
....
....
....

Worries I need to share with You. . .
....
....
....
....
....

I am overwhelmed. . .

....

....

....

....

I need Your strength. . .

....

....

....

....

Please give me wisdom. . .

....

....

....

....

....

....

Amen. Thank You, Father, for hearing my prayers.

*And God is able to bless you abundantly, so that
in all things at all times, having all that you need,
you will abound in every good work.*

2 CORINTHIANS 9:8

Date:

Dear Heavenly Father,
....
....
....
....

My prayer for my kid(s) today. . .
....
....
....
....
....
....
....
....
....

Thank You for. . .
....
....
....
....
....
....
....
....
....
....

Worries I need to share with You. . .
....
....
....
....
....

I am overwhelmed. . .

I need Your strength. . .

Please give me wisdom. . .

Amen. Thank You, Father, for hearing my prayers.

Is anyone among you in trouble? Let them pray.
Is anyone happy? Let them sing songs of praise.
JAMES 5:13

Date:

Dear Heavenly Father,

My prayer for my kid(s) today. . .

Thank You for. . .

Worries I need to share with You. . .

I am overwhelmed. . .

....

....

....

....

I need Your strength. . .

....

....

....

....

Please give me wisdom. . .

....

....

....

....

....

Amen. Thank You, Father, for hearing my prayers.

*The LORD is my strength and my shield; my heart
trusts in him, and he helps me. My heart leaps
for joy, and with my song I praise him.*

PSALM 28:7

Date:

Dear Heavenly Father,
....
....
....
....

My prayer for my kid(s) today. . .
....
....
....
....
....
....
....
....
....
....

Thank You for. . .
....
....
....
....
....
....
....
....
....

Worries I need to share with You. . .
....
....
....
....
....

I am overwhelmed. . .

....
....
....

I need Your strength. . .

....
....
....
....

Please give me wisdom. . .

....
....
....
....
....

Amen. Thank You, Father, for hearing my prayers.

For what you have done I will always praise you
in the presence of your faithful people. And I will
hope in your name, for your name is good.
PSALM 52:9

Date: _____

Dear Heavenly Father, ...
....
....
....
....

My prayer for my kid(s) today. . .
....
....
....
....
....
....
....
....

Thank You for. . .
....
....
....
....
....
....
....
....

Worries I need to share with You. . .
....
....
....
....
....

I am overwhelmed. . .

I need Your strength. . .

Please give me wisdom. . .

Amen. Thank You, Father, for hearing my prayers.

A gentle answer turns away wrath.
PROVERBS 15:1

Date:

Dear Heavenly Father,
....
....
....
....

My prayer for my kid(s) today. . .
....
....
....
....
....
....
....
....

Thank You for. . .
....
....
....
....
....
....
....
....
....

Worries I need to share with You. . .
....
....
....
....
....

I am overwhelmed. . .

....
....
....
....

I need Your strength. . .

....
....
....
....

Please give me wisdom. . .

....
....
....
....

Amen. Thank You, Father, for hearing my prayers.

The LORD is good, a refuge in times of trouble.
He cares for those who trust in him.
NAHUM 1:7

Date:

Dear Heavenly Father,
....
....
....
....

My prayer for my kid(s) today. . .
....
....
....
....
....
....
....
....
....

Thank You for. . .
....
....
....
....
....
....
....
....
....

Worries I need to share with You. . .
....
....
....
....
....

I am overwhelmed. . .

I need Your strength. . .

Please give me wisdom. . .

Amen. Thank You, Father, for hearing my prayers.

When anxiety was great within me,
your consolation brought me joy.
PSALM 94:19

Date:

Dear Heavenly Father,
....
....
....
....

My prayer for my kid(s)
today. . .
....
....
....
....
....
....
....
....
....

Thank You for. . .
....
....
....
....
....
....
....
....
....
....

Worries I need to share with You. . .
....
....
....
....
....

I am overwhelmed. . .

....

....

....

....

I need Your strength. . .

....

....

....

....

Please give me wisdom. . .

....

....

....

....

....

....

Amen. Thank You, Father, for hearing my prayers.

In all my prayers for all of you,
I always pray with joy.
PHILIPPIANS 1:4

Date:

Dear Heavenly Father,
....
....
....
....

My prayer for my kid(s) today. . .
....
....
....
....
....
....
....
....
....

Thank You for. . .
....
....
....
....
....
....
....
....

Worries I need to share with You. . .
....
....
....
....
....

I am overwhelmed. . .

....

....

....

....

I need Your strength. . .

....

....

....

....

Please give me wisdom. . .

....

....

....

....

....

Amen. Thank You, Father, for hearing my prayers.

*And now, dear children, continue in him,
so that when he appears we may be confident
and unashamed before him at his coming.*

1 John 2:28

Date:

Dear Heavenly Father,
....
....
....
....

My prayer for my kid(s) today. . .
....
....
....
....
....
....
....
....

Thank You for. . .
....
....
....
....
....
....
....
....
....
....

Worries I need to share with You. . .
....
....
....
....
....

I am overwhelmed. . .

....

....

....

....

I need Your strength. . .

....

....

....

....

Please give me wisdom. . .

....

....

....

....

....

....

Amen. Thank You, Father, for hearing my prayers.

Do not be anxious about anything,
but in every situation, by prayer and petition,
with thanksgiving, present your requests to God.

PHILIPPIANS 4:6

Date: _____

Dear Heavenly Father, ...
....
....
....
....

My prayer for my kid(s) today. . .
....
....
....
....
....
....
....
....

Thank You for. . .
....
....
....
....
....
....
....

Worries I need to share with You. . .
....
....
....
....
....

I am overwhelmed. . .

....
....
....
....

I need Your strength. . .

....
....
....
....

Please give me wisdom. . .

....
....
....
....
....

Amen. Thank You, Father, for hearing my prayers.

*Let your conversation be always full of
grace, seasoned with salt, so that you
may know how to answer everyone.*
COLOSSIANS 4:6

Date: ....

Dear Heavenly Father,...................
....
....
....
....

My prayer for my kid(s) today. . .
....
....
....
....
....
....
....

Thank You for. . .
....
....
....
....
....
....
....

Worries I need to share with You. . .
....
....
....
....
....

I am overwhelmed. . .

....

....

....

I need Your strength. . .

....

....

....

....

Please give me wisdom. . .

....

....

....

....

....

Amen. Thank You, Father, for hearing my prayers.

Whoever fears the LORD has a secure fortress,
and for their children it will be a refuge.
PROVERBS 14:26

Date:

Dear Heavenly Father,
....
....
....
....

My prayer for my kid(s) today. . .
....
....
....
....
....
....
....
....

Thank You for. . .
....
....
....
....
....
....
....
....
....

Worries I need to share with You. . .
....
....
....
....
....

I am overwhelmed. . .

....
....
....
....

I need Your strength. . .

....
....
....
....

Please give me wisdom. . .

....
....
....
....
....
....

Amen. Thank You, Father, for hearing my prayers.

Be strong and take heart,
all you who hope in the LORD.
PSALM 31:24

Date:

Dear Heavenly Father,

My prayer for my kid(s) today. . .

Thank You for. . .

Worries I need to share with You. . .

I am overwhelmed. . .

I need Your strength. . .

Please give me wisdom. . .

Amen. Thank You, Father, for hearing my prayers.

All Scripture is God-breathed and is useful
for teaching, rebuking, correcting
and training in righteousness.
2 TIMOTHY 3:16

Date:

Dear Heavenly Father,
....
....
....
....

My prayer for my kid(s)
today. . .
....
....
....
....
....
....
....
....
....

Thank You for. . .
....
....
....
....
....
....
....
....
....

Worries I need to share with You. . .
....
....
....
....
....

I am overwhelmed. . .

I need Your strength. . .

Please give me wisdom. . .

Amen. Thank You, Father, for hearing my prayers.

So in Christ Jesus you are all
children of God through faith.

GALATIANS 3:26

Date:

Dear Heavenly Father, ...
....
....
....
....

My prayer for my kid(s)
today. . .
....
....
....
....
....
....
....
....
....
....
....
....

Thank You for. . .
....
....
....
....
....
....
....
....
....
....
....

Worries I need to share with You. . .
....
....
....
....
....

I am overwhelmed. . .

I need Your strength. . .

Please give me wisdom. . .

Amen. Thank You, Father, for hearing my prayers.

You, Lord, are forgiving and good,
abounding in love to all who call to you.
PSALM 86:5

Date:

Dear Heavenly Father,

My prayer for my kid(s) today. . .

Thank You for. . .

Worries I need to share with You. . .

I am overwhelmed. . .

_____

_____

_____

_____

I need Your strength. . .

_____

_____

_____

_____

Please give me wisdom. . .

_____

_____

_____

_____

_____

_____

Amen. Thank You, Father, for hearing my prayers.

Trust in the Lord with all your heart and
lean not on your own understanding.
PROVERBS 3:5

Date:

Dear Heavenly Father,
....
....
....
....

My prayer for my kid(s)
today. . .
....
....
....
....
....
....
....
....

Thank You for. . .
....
....
....
....
....
....
....
....

Worries I need to share with You. . .
....
....
....
....
....

I am overwhelmed. . .

....

....

....

....

I need Your strength. . .

....

....

....

....

Please give me wisdom. . .

....

....

....

....

....

Amen. Thank You, Father, for hearing my prayers.

I sought the LORD, and he answered me;
he delivered me from all my fears.
PSALM 34:4

Date:

Dear Heavenly Father,
....
....
....
....

My prayer for my kid(s) today. . .
....
....
....
....
....
....
....
....
....
....
....

Thank You for. . .
....
....
....
....
....
....
....
....
....

Worries I need to share with You. . .
....
....
....
....
....

I am overwhelmed. . .

I need Your strength. . .

Please give me wisdom. . .

Amen. Thank You, Father, for hearing my prayers.

*He tends his flock like a shepherd: He gathers
the lambs in his arms and carries them close to
his heart; he gently leads those that have young.*

ISAIAH 40:11

Date:

Dear Heavenly Father,
....
....
....
....

My prayer for my kid(s) today. . .
....
....
....
....
....
....
....
....

Thank You for. . .
....
....
....
....
....
....
....
....

Worries I need to share with You. . .
....
....
....
....
....

I am overwhelmed. . .

I need Your strength. . .

Please give me wisdom. . .

Amen. Thank You, Father, for hearing my prayers.

And my God will meet all your needs according
to the riches of his glory in Christ Jesus.
PHILIPPIANS 4:19

Date:

Dear Heavenly Father,

My prayer for my kid(s) today. . .

Thank You for. . .

Worries I need to share with You. . .

I am overwhelmed. . .

I need Your strength. . .

Please give me wisdom. . .

Amen. Thank You, Father, for hearing my prayers.

*But you, Lord, are a compassionate
and gracious God, slow to anger,
abounding in love and faithfulness.*
PSALM 86:15

Date:

Dear Heavenly Father,

My prayer for my kid(s)
today. . .

Thank You for. . .

Worries I need to share with You. . .

I am overwhelmed. . .

....

....

....

....

I need Your strength. . .

....

....

....

....

Please give me wisdom. . .

....

....

....

....

....

....

Amen. Thank You, Father, for hearing my prayers.

I cry to you, LORD; I say, "You are my refuge,
my portion in the land of the living."
PSALM 142:5

Date:

Dear Heavenly Father,
....
....
....
....

My prayer for my kid(s) today. . .
....
....
....
....
....
....
....
....
....
....

Thank You for. . .
....
....
....
....
....
....
....
....
....

Worries I need to share with You. . .
....
....
....
....
....

I am overwhelmed. . .

....

....

....

I need Your strength. . .

....

....

....

....

Please give me wisdom. . .

....

....

....

....

....

....

Amen. Thank You, Father, for hearing my prayers.

*Always giving thanks to God the Father for
everything, in the name of our Lord Jesus Christ.*
EPHESIANS 5:20

Date:

Dear Heavenly Father,
....
....
....
....

My prayer for my kid(s) today. . .
....
....
....
....
....
....
....
....
....
....

Thank You for. . .
....
....
....
....
....
....
....
....

Worries I need to share with You. . .
....
....
....
....
....

I am overwhelmed. . .

....

....

....

I need Your strength. . .

....

....

....

....

Please give me wisdom. . .

....

....

....

....

....

....

Amen. Thank You, Father, for hearing my prayers.

Praise be to the Lord, to God our Savior,
who daily bears our burdens.
PSALM 68:19

Dear Heavenly Father,

My prayer for my kid(s) today. . .

Thank You for. . .

Worries I need to share with You. . .

I am overwhelmed. . .

_____

_____

_____

_____

I need Your strength. . .

_____

_____

_____

_____

Please give me wisdom. . .

_____

_____

_____

_____

_____

_____

Amen. Thank You, Father, for hearing my prayers.

The prospect of the righteous is joy.

PROVERBS 10:28

Date:

Dear Heavenly Father,

My prayer for my kid(s) today. . .

Thank You for. . .

Worries I need to share with You. . .

I am overwhelmed. . .

_____
_____
_____
_____

I need Your strength. . .

_____
_____
_____
_____

Please give me wisdom. . .

_____
_____
_____
_____

Amen. Thank You, Father, for hearing my prayers.

"But blessed is the one who trusts in
the Lord, whose confidence is in him."
JEREMIAH 17:7

Date:

Dear Heavenly Father,..
....
....
....
....

My prayer for my kid(s) today. . .
....
....
....
....
....
....
....

Thank You for. . .
....
....
....
....
....
....
....
....
....
....

Worries I need to share with You. . .
....
....
....
....
....

I am overwhelmed. . .

....

....

....

I need Your strength. . .

....

....

....

....

Please give me wisdom. . .

....

....

....

....

....

Amen. Thank You, Father, for hearing my prayers.

May the God of hope fill you with all joy and peace
as you trust in him, so that you may overflow
with hope by the power of the Holy Spirit.
ROMANS 15:13

Date:

Dear Heavenly Father,
....
....
....
....

My prayer for my kid(s) today. . .
....
....
....
....
....
....
....

Thank You for. . .
....
....
....
....
....
....
....
....
....

Worries I need to share with You. . .
....
....
....
....
....

I am overwhelmed. . .

_____
_____
_____
_____

I need Your strength. . .

_____
_____
_____
_____

Please give me wisdom. . .

_____
_____
_____
_____
_____
_____

Amen. Thank You, Father, for hearing my prayers.

As for me, I will always have hope;
I will praise you more and more.
PSALM 71:14

Date:

Dear Heavenly Father,

My prayer for my kid(s) today. . .

Thank You for. . .

Worries I need to share with You. . .

I am overwhelmed. . .

I need Your strength. . .

Please give me wisdom. . .

Amen. Thank You, Father, for hearing my prayers.

Let us hold unswervingly to the hope we profess,
for he who promised is faithful.
HEBREWS 10:23

Date:

Dear Heavenly Father,

My prayer for my kid(s) today. . .

Thank You for. . .

Worries I need to share with You. . .

I am overwhelmed. . .

I need Your strength. . .

Please give me wisdom. . .

Amen. Thank You, Father, for hearing my prayers.

A cheerful heart is good medicine.
PROVERBS 17:22

Date:

Dear Heavenly Father,..
....
....
....
....

My prayer for my kid(s) today...
....
....
....
....
....
....
....
....

Thank You for...
....
....
....
....
....
....
....
....
....

Worries I need to share with You...
....
....
....
....
....

I am overwhelmed. . .

....

....

....

....

I need Your strength. . .

....

....

....

....

Please give me wisdom. . .

....

....

....

....

....

Amen. Thank You, Father, for hearing my prayers.

May your unfailing love be with us,
LORD, even as we put our hope in you.
PSALM 33:22

Date:

Dear Heavenly Father,
....
....
....
....

My prayer for my kid(s) today. . .
....
....
....
....
....
....
....
....
....
....

Thank You for. . .
....
....
....
....
....
....
....
....

Worries I need to share with You. . .
....
....
....
....
....

I am overwhelmed. . .

I need Your strength. . .

Please give me wisdom. . .

Amen. Thank You, Father, for hearing my prayers.

Whatever you have learned or received or heard
from me, or seen in me—put it into practice.
And the God of peace will be with you.

PHILIPPIANS 4:9

Date:

Dear Heavenly Father,

My prayer for my kid(s) today. . .

Thank You for. . .

Worries I need to share with You. . .

I am overwhelmed. . .

....

....

....

I need Your strength. . .

....

....

....

Please give me wisdom. . .

....

....

....

....

....

....

Amen. Thank You, Father, for hearing my prayers.

For you have been my hope, Sovereign LORD,
my confidence since my youth.

PSALM 71:5

Date:

Dear Heavenly Father,
....
....
....
....

My prayer for my kid(s) today. . .
....
....
....
....
....
....
....

Thank You for. . .
....
....
....
....
....
....
....
....

Worries I need to share with You. . .
....
....
....
....
....

I am overwhelmed. . .

....

....

....

....

I need Your strength. . .

....

....

....

....

Please give me wisdom. . .

....

....

....

....

....

....

Amen. Thank You, Father, for hearing my prayers.

"Blessed rather are those who hear
the word of God and obey it."
LUKE 11:28

Date:

Dear Heavenly Father,
....
....
....
....

My prayer for my kid(s) today...
....
....
....
....
....
....
....
....

Thank You for...
....
....
....
....
....
....
....
....
....
....

Worries I need to share with You...
....
....
....
....
....

I am overwhelmed. . .

I need Your strength. . .

Please give me wisdom. . .

Amen. Thank You, Father, for hearing my prayers.

*And the Lord's servant must. . .be kind
to everyone, able to teach, not resentful.*
2 TIMOTHY 2:24

Date:

Dear Heavenly Father,

My prayer for my kid(s) today...

Thank You for...

Worries I need to share with You...

I am overwhelmed. . .

....

....

....

....

I need Your strength. . .

....

....

....

....

Please give me wisdom. . .

....

....

....

....

....

....

Amen. Thank You, Father, for hearing my prayers.

Be alert and of sober mind
so that you may pray.
1 PETER 4:7

Date:

Dear Heavenly Father,

....
....
....
....

My prayer for my kid(s) today...

....
....
....
....
....
....
....
....

Thank You for...

....
....
....
....
....
....
....
....

Worries I need to share with You...

....
....
....
....
....

I am overwhelmed. . .

I need Your strength. . .

Please give me wisdom. . .

Amen. Thank You, Father, for hearing my prayers.

Praise the LORD. Praise the LORD, my soul.
I will praise the LORD all my life; I will sing
praise to my God as long as I live.

PSALM 146:1–2

Date:

Dear Heavenly Father,
....
....
....
....

My prayer for my kid(s)
today. . .
....
....
....
....
....
....
....
....
....
....

Thank You for. . .
....
....
....
....
....
....
....
....
....

Worries I need to share with You. . .
....
....
....
....
....

I am overwhelmed. . .

....
....
....
....

I need Your strength. . .

....
....
....
....

Please give me wisdom. . .

....
....
....
....
....
....

Amen. Thank You, Father, for hearing my prayers.

*You will keep in perfect peace those whose minds
are steadfast, because they trust in you.*
ISAIAH 26:3

Date:

Dear Heavenly Father,

My prayer for my kid(s) today. . .

Thank You for. . .

Worries I need to share with You. . .

I am overwhelmed. . .

....

....

....

....

I need Your strength. . .

....

....

....

....

Please give me wisdom. . .

....

....

....

....

....

Amen. Thank You, Father, for hearing my prayers.

I wait for the LORD, my whole being waits,
and in his word I put my hope.
PSALM 130:5

Date:

Dear Heavenly Father,
....
....
....
....

My prayer for my kid(s) today. . .
....
....
....
....
....
....
....
....
....
....

Thank You for. . .
....
....
....
....
....
....
....
....
....
....
....

Worries I need to share with You. . .
....
....
....
....
....

I am overwhelmed. . .

_____

_____

_____

_____

I need Your strength. . .

_____

_____

_____

_____

Please give me wisdom. . .

_____

_____

_____

_____

_____

Amen. Thank You, Father, for hearing my prayers.

As Scripture says, "Anyone who believes
in him will never be put to shame."
ROMANS 10:11

Date:

Dear Heavenly Father,
....
....
....
....

My prayer for my kid(s) today. . .
....
....
....
....
....
....
....
....
....
....
....

Thank You for. . .
....
....
....
....
....
....
....
....

Worries I need to share with You. . .
....
....
....
....
....

I am overwhelmed. . .

I need Your strength. . .

Please give me wisdom. . .

Amen. Thank You, Father, for hearing my prayers.

*"Peace I leave with you; my peace I give you.
I do not give to you as the world gives. Do not
let your hearts be troubled and do not be afraid."*

JOHN 14:27

Date:

Dear Heavenly Father,...
....
....
....
....

My prayer for my kid(s) today. . .
....
....
....
....
....
....
....
....
....

Thank You for. . .
....
....
....
....
....
....
....
....
....

Worries I need to share with You. . .
....
....
....
....
....

I am overwhelmed. . .

I need Your strength. . .

Please give me wisdom. . .

Amen. Thank You, Father, for hearing my prayers.

Great peace have those who love your law,
and nothing can make them stumble.
PSALM 119:165

Date:

Dear Heavenly Father,...
....
....
....
....

My prayer for my kid(s) today. . .
....
....
....
....
....
....
....
....

Thank You for. . .
....
....
....
....
....
....
....

Worries I need to share with You. . .
....
....
....
....
....

I am overwhelmed. . .

....
....
....
....

I need Your strength. . .

....
....
....
....

Please give me wisdom. . .

....
....
....
....
....
....

Amen. Thank You, Father, for hearing my prayers.

"The grass withers and the flowers fall,
but the word of our God endures forever."
ISAIAH 40:8

Date:

Dear Heavenly Father,
....
....
....
....

My prayer for my kid(s)
today. . .
....
....
....
....
....
....
....
....
....
....

Thank You for. . .
....
....
....
....
....
....
....
....
....

Worries I need to share with You. . .
....
....
....
....
....

I am overwhelmed. . .

....
....
....
....

I need Your strength. . .

....
....
....
....

Please give me wisdom. . .

....
....
....
....
....
....

Amen. Thank You, Father, for hearing my prayers.

"The eternal God is your refuge,
and underneath are the everlasting arms."
DEUTERONOMY 33:27

Date:

Dear Heavenly Father,
....
....
....
....

My prayer for my kid(s)
today. . .
....
....
....
....
....
....
....

Thank You for. . .
....
....
....
....
....
....
....
....
....

Worries I need to share with You. . .
....
....
....
....
....

I am overwhelmed. . .

I need Your strength. . .

Please give me wisdom. . .

Amen. Thank You, Father, for hearing my prayers.

"Blessed are the pure in heart,
for they will see God."
MATTHEW 5:8

Date:

Dear Heavenly Father,
....
....
....
....
....

My prayer for my kid(s) today. . .
....
....
....
....
....
....
....
....
....
....

Thank You for. . .
....
....
....
....
....
....
....
....
....

Worries I need to share with You. . .
....
....
....
....
....

I am overwhelmed. . .

I need Your strength. . .

Please give me wisdom. . .

Amen. Thank You, Father, for hearing my prayers.

"Ask and it will be given to you; seek and you will find;
knock and the door will be opened to you. For everyone
who asks receives; the one who seeks finds; and to
the one who knocks, the door will be opened."

MATTHEW 7:7–8

Date: ....

Dear Heavenly Father,..
....
....
....
....

My prayer for my kid(s) today. . .
....
....
....
....
....
....
....
....
....

Thank You for. . .
....
....
....
....
....
....
....
....
....

Worries I need to share with You. . .
....
....
....
....
....

I am overwhelmed. . .

I need Your strength. . .

Please give me wisdom. . .

Amen. Thank You, Father, for hearing my prayers.

Answer me when I call to you,
my righteous God.
PSALM 4:1

Date:

Dear Heavenly Father,..

....

....

....

Thank You for. . .

....

....

....

....

....

....

....

....

My prayer for my kid(s) today. . .

....

....

....

....

....

....

....

....

Worries I need to share with You. . .

....

....

....

....

....

I am overwhelmed. . .

I need Your strength. . .

Please give me wisdom. . .

Amen. Thank You, Father, for hearing my prayers.

*Like newborn babies, crave pure spiritual milk,
so that by it you may grow up in your salvation,
now that you have tasted that the Lord is good.*

1 PETER 2:2–3

Date:

Dear Heavenly Father, ...
....
....
....
....

Thank You for...
....
....
....
....
....
....
....
....
....

My prayer for my kid(s) today...
....
....
....
....
....
....
....
....
....

Worries I need to share with You...
....
....
....
....
....

I am overwhelmed. . .

....

....

....

....

I need Your strength. . .

....

....

....

....

Please give me wisdom. . .

....

....

....

....

....

Amen. Thank You, Father, for hearing my prayers.

Pray continually.
1 Thessalonians 5:17

THE PRAYER MAP®
FOR THE ENTIRE FAMILY. . .

The Prayer Map for Men
978-1-64352-438-2

The Prayer Map for Women
978-1-68322-557-7

The Prayer Map for Girls
978-1-68322-559-1

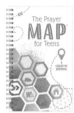

The Prayer Map for Boys
978-1-68322-558-4

The Prayer Map for Teens
978-1-68322-556-0

These purposeful prayer journals are a fun and creative way to more fully experience the power of prayer. Each page guides you to write out thoughts, ideas, and lists. . .which then creates a specific "map" for you to follow as you talk to God. Each map includes a spot to record the date, so you can look back on your prayers and see how God has worked in your life. *The Prayer Map* will not only encourage you to spend time talking with God about the things that matter most. . .it will also help you build a healthy spiritual habit of continual prayer for life!

Spiral Bound / $7.99